Jim Spencer Broadbent & Johnjoe Irwin

Poppies

Salamander Street

PLAYS

First published in 2026 by Salamander Street Ltd., a Wordville imprint. (info@salamanderstreet.com).

Cover photography by Lu Guertler

ISBN: 9781066622924

10 9 8 7 6 5 4 3 2 1

Further copies of this publication can be purchased from www.salamanderstreet.com

"Beautiful Piece of Work"

⋆ ⋆ ⋆ ⋆ **The Peg**

"The play engages the audience with debate, humour and thought provoking writing"

⋆ ⋆ ⋆ ⋆ **Theatre Weekly**

"A raucous and illuminating theatrical experience"
"A compelling piece of theatre, rich in both ingenuity and heart"

⋆ ⋆ ⋆ ⋆ **Broadway Baby**

"An entertaining triumph that forces the audience to confront their latent biases."

⋆ ⋆ ⋆ ⋆ **London Fringe Theatre Reviews.**

ACKNOWLEDGEMENTS

GAIT productions would like to formally acknowledge and thank the following organisations;

Theatre Peckham for initially providing GAIT with in kind rehearsal space as part of 'Incubate Scheme', Omnibus Theatre for involvement in both 'Omniwright' and for in-kind rehearsal space to prepare for their scratch night 'Engine Room', Camden People's Theatre for providing us with the opportunity to be part of their annual SPRINT festival and Greenwich Theatre for providing us with in-kind rehearsal space and programming as part of their 'See New Next Tuesday' season. Jim and Johnjoe would also like to thank the plethora of friends and family who have provided support and feedback to help *Poppies* reach its full potential.

Thank you / Míle buíochas.

Jim Spencer Broadbent & Johnjoe Irwin
2026

INTRODUCTION

Poppies is the result of years of theatre making both across Ireland and England and how these two individuals interact with each other because of their identity and heritage. It was written at a time when Union Jacks and St George's crosses were being put up in England and the Irish tricolour was being put up across Ireland with anti-immigration sentiments at the heart of both, when the British Government and military continue to be complicit in colonialism and genocide through direct and indirect support of atrocities being committed across the globe. Johnjoe and Jim are based on real people; two men in their late twenties who lived together in South-East London.

> 'And if there ever is gonna be healing
> There has to be remembering
> And then grieving
> So that there can be forgiving
> There has to be knowledge and understanding'
> — Sinéad O'Connor, *Famine*

Jim Spencer Broadbent & Johnjoe Irwin
2026

Poppies was first presented at Camden People's Theatre, London on 27th of March 2026 as part of their annual SPRINT Festival. The piece was written by and performed by Jim Spencer Broadbent & Johnjoe Irwin as part of GAIT Productions. The cast was as follows:

Jim	**Jim Spencer Broadbent**
Johnjoe	**Johnjoe Irwin**

CREATIVE TEAM

Jim Spencer Broadbent | Writer/Performer

Jim is an Essex-born playwright. His work identifies and explores surreality within contemporary ideas and practices. His fast-paced, physical style has earned previous work four-star reviews for both writing and performing. He is the co-creator of *Poppies*.

Johnjoe Irwin | Writer/Performer

Johnjoe is a professionally trained actor and writer from Dublin, Ireland. He graduated from the MA in Actor and Performer Training at Rose Bruford College, London, with a distinction and has also trained with the Gaiety School of Acting, Dublin, as part of the Advanced Performance Course.

He is an avid storyteller and has a keen interest in Site Specific and Immersive work that blurs the line between stage and audience. His previous work and performances have garnered an OFFCOM Commendation, an OFFEST Nomination and multiple five-star reviews. He is the co-creator of *Poppies*.

Cian Feasey | Lighting Designer/Programmer

Cian Feasey is a half-English, half-Irish Lighting Designer from South-East London. He has a deep passion for theatre and communicating a story, through the medium of lighting. This play speaks to Cian on a deeper level, as someone who comes from both backgrounds and sometimes wrestles with his identity surrounding British and Irish heritage

Lu Guertler | Photographer of Cover Image:

Any disciplines not listed above were completed by co-creators of the piece.

Jim Spencer Broadbent & Johnjoe Irwin

Poppies

CHARACTERS

JIM

mid to late 20s, English

JOHNJOE

mid to late 20s, Irish

NOTES FROM THE WRITERS

Scenes oftentimes blend into one another. A '/' indicates an interruption.

The play was originally performed with minimal set design; a sofa centre stage, one mannequin stage left, one mannequin stage right. One has a button that reads 'POPPY' the other has one that reads 'NOT A POPPY'. Four white boxes; two in front of the sofa to make a coffee table and two either side of the sofa. There is half a packet of Custard Cream Biscuits and a vase with flowers in it on this makeshift coffee table. Any set up that portrays these three spaces; Realism, Surrealism & Direct Address will suffice.

The ending described in this edition was formulated by Jim Spencer Broadbent and Johnjoe Irwin and can be altered by any new creative team.

1: BEGINNING OF THE PLAY

Lights up.

Performers enter from opposite sides of the stage slowly. Both walk towards the mannequins and inspect them.

JOHNJOE replaces the 'NOT A POPPY BADGE' with a 'POPPY' badge.

They look at each other.

JIM: Shall we?

JOHNJOE: Sure.

JIM: Ready.

JOHNJOE: Set.

BOTH: Go.

A change in lighting state. A lighting state that is to be repeated for 'Middle of the Play' and 'End of the Play'. Performers address audience directly.

JOHNJOE: Hello.

JIM: Hello.

JOHNJOE: I'm Johnjoe.

JIM: I'm Jim.

BOTH: And we're best friends.

JIM: You might be here for

BOTH: Political theatre.

JOHNJOE: Which it is in some ways.

JIM: But if you're not interested in

BOTH: Political theatre.

JOHNJOE: Don't worry. The play isn't just that.

JIM: It's also about.

BOTH: Men's mental health.

JIM: In this piece we have a big conversation.

JOHNJOE: And you might think it's strange.

JIM: But it's how we talk to each other.

JOHNJOE: Land on the sofa.

JIM: After a few beers.

JOHNJOE: And chat the night away.

JIM: About things we have in common.

JOHNJOE: About how we're different.

JIM: He's Irish.

JOHNJOE: He's English.

BOTH: This is not an Irish English play.

JIM: There's so much more nuance to it than that.

JOHNJOE: At the start, I didn't like Jim because he did my accent within the first five minutes of meeting me.

JIM: At the start, I didn't like Johnjoe because he didn't appreciate my perfect Dublin accent. But I think we're over that now.

JOHNJOE: That moment will never leave me.

JIM: He taught me an awful lot about British History in Ireland.

JOHNJOE: Oh boy, did we take the piss out of him.

JIM: Such a supportive, learning environment.

JOHNJOE: But now he's aware of things he was never taught.

JIM: I'm now aware of things I was never taught.

BOTH: Which is important.

JIM: This is a story about my identity.

JOHNJOE: This is a story about my identity.

BOTH: And how it's stronger now than ever before.

JIM: That being said, it's been a while since we've really got into it.

JOHNJOE: And nothing's changed.

JIM: And everything's changed.

JOHNJOE: What's important.

JIM: Is that.

JOHNJOE: We're still absolutely.

JIM: Utterly.

JOHNJOE: And without a doubt.

BOTH: On the same page. Enjoy the show!

2: FRIENDSHIP IS REALISM

A change in lighting state; Realism. JIM is writing on a Birthday card..

JOHNJOE: Hey, man.

JIM: Oi oi! I didn't know you were in.

JOHNJOE: Just got back, and I made you a cup of tea.

JIM: Ah, magnifique.

JOHNJOE: Sláinte, bud.

JIM: Cheers, geez.

BOTH take a sip.

JIM: Now that's a lovely brew.

JOHNJOE: That's because it's Irish tea, not bad tea.

JIM: We've been through this, you can't just call English tea bad tea.

JOHNJOE: Yes I can, it's factual. Same with butter; Irish butter is just far superior to English butter.

JIM: Tea is our thing!

JOHNJOE: The Chinese invented tea, Jim.

JIM: I'm not saying we invented it, but it's our thing now, undoubtedly.

JOHNJOE: Classic Brit, claiming something else that doesn't belong to you. That's your thing.

JIM: That's my shirt.

Pause.

JOHNJOE: Reparations.

JIM: What've you been up to today?

JOHNJOE: Just picking some bits up from Georgia's.

JIM: Tough.

JOHNJOE: Wouldn't have been if the trains were running the way they're meant to.

JIM: A couple of leaves on the tracks and it all falls to pieces.

JOHNJOE: Tell me about it.

JIM: Sorry mate.

JOHNJOE: That's almost the lot of it now though so should be done.

JIM: The final death.

JIM laughs. JOHNJOE doesn't.

JOHNJOE: Yep.
What were you up to?

JIM: Oh, just writing.

JOHNJOE: I never knew you wrote by hand.

JIM: Oh, this isn't a theatre thing.

JOHNJOE: I was about to say that doesn't seem very efficient.

JIM: I'm writing to someone.

JOHNJOE: Who?

Pause.

JIM: Is it alright if I don't wanna say?

JOHNJOE: What?

JIM: I just don't want to say.

JOHNJOE: Wait. Do you have some kind of romantic pen pal?

JIM: No!

JOHNJOE: That's so cute!

JIM: No! You weren't even meant to see this, I thought you were at work tonight.

JOHNJOE: I wasn't meant to see what?

JIM: Nothing!

JOHNJOE: Why are you being so weird?

JIM: I just don't want to have a big conversation about it right now.

JOHNJOE: A big conversation? Who are you writing to?

JIM: You're gonna get weird!

JOHNJOE: I'm not gonna get weird.

JIM: You are.

JOHNJOE: I promise I'm not.

JIM: I know you.

JOHNJOE: Then you know I'm not going to let this go.

JIM: I'm writing to a veteran.

Pause.

JIM: Told you. Weird.

JOHNJOE: I'm not being weird!

JIM: Then why the silence?

JOHNJOE: I'm just processing it, that's all.

JIM: What are you processing, exactly?

JOHNJOE: Like, is this something you do regularly?

JIM: No.

JOHNJOE: Can I see?

JIM: No.

JOHNJOE: Why? Did you sign it off with a kiss?

JIM: No!
Just leave it man.

JOHNJOE: Seriously, I don't get it. Is he related to you?

JIM: No. Well… not by blood.

JOHNJOE: What the hell does that mean, not by blood?

JIM: I saw this thing on the news. Former member of the Navy, Dougie Telley is celebrating his 100th birthday. He was at D-Day.

JOHNJOE: Alright, what's that got to do with you?

JIM: Just watch.

The voice of a news programme and veteran Dougie Telley, is heard or projected.

NEWS V/O: The RAF Fourth regiment of Southend on Sea are calling out for birthday cards for the D-Day veteran, to make his birthday extra special.

DOUGIE V/O: "There's not many of us around anymore, and if I was to make it to a hundred, I'd be so lucky."

JIM: Don't you think that's just amazing?

JOHNJOE: Sure I guess. But what's that got to do with you?

JIM: He's from Southend. Like me

JOHNJOE: Lots of people are from Southend Jim.

JIM: His birthday?

JOHNJOE: It's not uncommon for people to live over a hundred nowadays.

JIM: Not that.

JOHNJOE: Then what?

JIM: October. October 23rd.

Pause.

JOHNJOE looks at JIM blankly and JIM looks back in disbelief. It finally clicks for JOHNJOE.

JOHNJOE: That's your birthday!

JIM: You're such a bad mate

JOHNJOE: I'm bad with dates!

JIM: You're bad with friendship.

JOHNJOE: Still, so what?

JIM: I'm just saying, it hit home a bit for me.

JOHNJOE: Made what hit home?

JIM: That could have been me. Like, if I was born 72 years earlier then I would have been made to fight for my country.

JOHNJOE: You don't know that he was made to do anything, not every young man was conscripted.

JIM: I think it's safe to assume.

JOHNJOE: Not necessarily.

JIM: That's beside the point. Here he sits, at 100 years old with no living family or friends to celebrate with. He was at D-Day you know?

JOHNJOE: Yeah. You mentioned.

JIM goes to speak but holds back.

JOHNJOE: What?

JIM: No, nothing.

JOHNJOE: What were you going to say?

JIM: I can feel you gearing up to go all republican on me.

JOHNJOE: Wow, OK! You know that I'm not a huge fan of British Army Veterans, Jim, understandably so I think.

JIM: I know but this is different. D-Day was different.

JOHNJOE: Yeah, the one time you were on the right side of history.

JIM: Yeah exactly, so is it not alright that I write to an old lonely man on his birthday.

Is that OK? Do I have to ask permission to do such a thing?

JOHNJOE: No, of course not. I'm just messin'. It's fine, you do you.

3: ASSEMBLY IS SURREALISM

A change in lighting state; Surrealism.

A school bell rings.

The shift between these two scenes is immediate JOHNJOE plays MR IRWIN and JIM plays MR BROADBENT.

BOTH go to their mannequins and put the blazers on. BOTH have a badge that reads 'POPPY' on the blazer.

IRWIN: Thank you Mr Broadbent for a wonderful presentation. Final few bits. Is there a ______________ in attendance?

Audience Participation.

The staff cohort are aware of your Facebook page where you rate us from 'fit to fugly'. Those posts are to be taken down immediately, thank you.

Sir?

BROADBENT: I would like to encourage everyone in the room today to congratulate the year nine rugby team's tremendous victory in the Essex Cup Final last weekend with a round of applause.

The audience applauds.

IRWIN: Yes absolutely, Sir. However, it is because of events that transpired during that game of rugby that PC Cooper will be taking Wednesday's assembly to talk to you all about the dangers of mob mentality and joint enterprise.

OK, wonderful. Let's not keep you any longer than we/

BROADBENT: /Sorry, Sir, Permission slips for Ypres.

IRWIN: Yes! Thank you for reminding me, Sir. We need those slips from your parents as soon as possible/

BROADBENT: /By Wednesday.

IRWIN: By Wednesday or you're not going guys. Simple as that.

BROADBENT: While we're on that, there are going to be lots of other schools from all over the country in these spaces at the same time as us and I want us to be the most respectful of the lot. Can we have you all practice your somber faces quickly? That's very good, thank you. I want there to be no doubt that our school truly grasps the scale of the tragedy of Ypres. Which clearly, we are currently failing.

Directed towards the audience.

Young man, could you get up here please.

BOTH bring an audience member onstage.

IRWIN: What's your name?

Pause. Wait for Audience participation.

And where, may I ask, is your poppy? C'mon? I mean it. Where is your poppy?

If the audience member speaks, the performers cut them off.

Now is not the time for excuses!

BROADBENT: We do not care where your poppy is. We are more concerned about where it isn't, and that's on your chest.

IRWIN: Look out at your peers, young man.

BROADBENT: Every other person in this hall is wearing a poppy. Why are they doing that sir?

IRWIN: To respect those that gave their lives to save the world from…

BOTH: The Nazis!

BROADBENT: Do you support the Nazis, young man?

IRWIN: Do you like the Nazis, young man?

BROADBENT: Because that is precisely what you are saying by not wearing a poppy.

IRWIN: This is exactly the type of insubordination that we will not accept next week in Belgium.

BROADBENT: It is the first week of November, guys. We have always said if you are not showing your respect for the war effort by now, you are displaying your selfishness, alongside a blatant disregard for our history.

IRWIN: Both values which this school will not stand by.

BROADBENT: Please take your seat.

The performers direct the audience member back to their seat.

MR BROADBENT is clearly distraught.

IRWIN: If that poppy is not on tomorrow it will be a morning in Isolation. You Understand? Good, wonderful.
Oh look.
You've upset Sir. Are you alright, Sir?

BROADBENT: I'm fine.

Beat.

BOTH: Chicken dippers and chips for lunch! Woo!

IRWIN: Great assembly.

BROADBENT: What a buzz.

BOTH: The curriculum is perfect. Fuck yeah!

A Bell rings.

4: FRIENDSHIP IS REALISM AGAIN

The school bell rings again.

The shift between these two scenes is immediate.

A change in lighting state; back to Realism.

PERFORMERS take off their blazers, place them on the mannequins and turn back into their former characters, JIM & JOHNJOE

JOHNJOE: That's insane.

JIM: It was always, if you do not wear a poppy, you're in isolation for the day.

JOHNJOE: Isolation?

JIM: You didn't have isolation? Basically if you misbehaved you had to sit at a desk facing the wall with wooden blinkers either side of you. You weren't allowed to speak or read or catch up with homework.

JOHNJOE: And was Miss Trunchible your headteacher?

JIM: Now I look back it was a bit much.

JOHNJOE: How were you meant to learn anything? Grow from your mistakes?

JIM: I don't think they really cared.

JOHNJOE: Did you ever get put into isolation?

JIM: Never. I was always pinned up a week in advance.

JOHNJOE: What a model student. You realise you didn't have to wear it.

JIM: You don't get it, if you didn't they'd go in on you. Honestly I heard all sorts; selfish horrible child, thankless brat.

JOHNJOE: Like Charli XCX?

JIM: Erm…

JOHNJOE: Do you reckon anyone's listened to Brat while wearing a poppy?

JIM: The odds are pretty high.

JOHNJOE: I don't know. It doesn't work with the whole aesthetic.

JIM: The colours kinda work.

JOHNJOE: The original Brat was not wearing a poppy at school.

JIM: There's something to it.

JOHNJOE: Brat not Brit.

BOTH: Woah.

JOHNJOE: These people were adults. Not just adults; educators at that.

JIM: It was the only thing we were ever allowed to celebrate.

JOHNJOE: It doesn't sound like it was ever celebrated, just enforced.

JIM: Don't get me wrong though, I wanted to wear one. It was the only thing that was ever simple.

JOHNJOE: But this is the thing. It never just represented something that simple.

JIM: That feeling, nobility.

JOHNJOE: Misplaced nobility.

JIM: Did you ever talk about it in assemblies?

JOHNJOE: Not really *(Laughs)*

Maybe… In a way.

JIM: What, why're you laughing?

JOHNJOE: It's just very very different. We were very different little boys.

JIM: We've always been different.

JOHNJOE: Yeah but…

I remember performing in one of them.

JIM: No way! You were an actor from day one!

JOHNJOE: I didn't act, I sang.

JIM: Oooh lah di da. I never knew you could sing!

JOHNJOE: I can't. It was more about the meaning behind the song.

JIM: What did you sing?

JOHNJOE: Would you like a rendition?

JIM: I would be honoured.

5: ASSEMBLY IN SURREALISM AGAIN

The shift between these two scenes is immediate.

A change in lighting state; Surrealism.

A loud assembly hall is heard. A primary school in Ireland. The blazers/badges are not worn.

BROADBENT: OK boys and girls I want you all to give a big clap of your hands for Johnjoe from second class with a lovely song for you all today.

JIM takes his place in the audience while JOHNJOE gets ready to perform.

JOHNJOE meanders to the stage, now a little boy, Young JJ.

YOUNG JJ: Some say the devil is dead,
the devil is dead, the devil is dead,
Some say the devil is dead and buried in Killarney.

JIM bursts out of his seat.

JIM: Oh I love it—how fun!

JJ holds up his finger and continues singing.

YOUNG JJ: More say he rose again,
More say he rose again,
More say he rose again,
And joined the British Army.

They both sit in it for a while. JIM meanders back onto stage.

6: FRIENDSHIP IS REALISM III

A change in lighting state; Realism.

The shift between these two scenes is immediate.

JOHNJOE: Oh, I'm sorry did eight year old me offend you?

JIM: Eight? That's just it. Like that hatred was there for you so early on.

JOHNJOE: Not sure it was outright hatred, more awareness of it, of what the British Army did in Ireland. My knowledge and your knowledge are worlds apart.

JIM: I know.

JOHNJOE: We were always aware of it, like it was in the air, you'd catch snippets of it from adults around you and not entirely understand it but, you'd feel it. This anger that's so visceral and so deep.

And then, in school we were taught about it.

all of it.

The Plantations, the 1798 rebellion, The Famine, The 1916
Rising, The War of Independence, The Troubles. And that's
just a snapshot into Ireland. People pushed off their land,
towns burned to the ground, our language and culture
outlawed.

How can this anger disappear when you refuse to reconcile, refuse to educate yourselves. When people like Soldier F are able to shoot civilians dead in the street during Bloody Sunday in Derry without consequence, without remorse. And still be let off. Still be supported until the bitter end.

And that's what the Poppy represents to me; It's colonialism and it's Empire and it's a refusal to change. It asks people to actively celebrate and support those who carried out atrocities in the name of domination and oppression. It supports all British veterans from all British wars.

JIM steps towards JOHNJOE.

JIM: It's good you get to be passionate about it, man. Good for you.

JOHNJOE: Yeah well, it got me into trouble.

My parents were brought in to speak to my principal about it. But we did get a Supermacs on the way home... so it was all a little confusing.

JIM: Supermacs? What's Supermacs?

JOHNJOE: Are you being serious right now? How many years in Dublin and you never got a Supermacs?

JIM: It's like McDonalds, right?

JOHNJOE: No! Not like McDonalds! I mean, OK yeah, it's an Irish fast food burger place so kind of like McDonald's... But they actually won a legal case against McDonalds to keep their name.

JIM: Right.

JOHNJOE: I don't think you're grasping how important this is. It was a modern day David vs Goliath story. McDonald's, this massive corporation tried to crush a small Irish chain and they lost! I actually think it's more relevant to this conversation than you realise.

JIM: OK, man, I get it.

JOHNJOE: No, you don't and you never will. God, they teach you nothing over here.

JIM: Chill out. You got a burger after being told off.

JOHNJOE: If you want to take all the history and heart out of it, then yes, I got a burger.

JIM: Felt like you were being rewarded?

JOHNJOE: A little yeah.

JIM: Like a little republican dog.

JOHNJOE: Ooh, not sure I'm in love with that wording.

JIM: Hungry for freedom.

JOHNJOE: I still am, man, I've got room for six more counties...

JIM: I've never rebelled against anything.

JOHNJOE: I know, you were so goddamn cute when we first met.

JIM: Leave it out!

JOHNJOE: You were though, you didn't have a clue. It was like you were a little lion cub.

JIM: What?

JOHNJOE: Given the chance to grow into a fully grown lion, you're scary, you're a killer but I caught you just in time to domesticate you.

JOHNJOE wrestles JIM in a brotherly way.

JIM: Get off me man!
I am a lion. A wild lion.

JOHNJOE: No, you're not, Jim! I nursed you with my Irish milk

JIM: I hate when you do this.

JOHNJOE: And now you're in my circus where I make you jump through hoops for custard creams.

JOHNJOE takes the custard creams from the coffee table and stands atop one of the boxes. He pretends to be a circus master.

JIM: Gimme one.

JOHNJOE: Say the thing.

JIM: I don't want to say it.

JOHNJOE: You want a custard cream, you'll say the thing.

Pause.

JIM: *(Quietly)* Tiocfaidh ár lá.

JOHNJOE: What was that? I couldn't make it out.

JIM: *(Louder)* Tiocfaidh ár lá.

JOHNJOE laughs and jumps off the chair

JOHNJOE: Good boy. That pronunciation has really come on leaps and bounds.

Pause.

Followed by continuous pauses.

JIM: I think I'm going to wear a poppy this year.

JOHNJOE: Right.

JIM: Just so you know. I thought I'd let you know.

JOHNJOE: I haven't seen you wear one before.

JIM: No, that's why I'm letting you know, innit.

JOHNJOE: Uh huh.

JIM: Being in the same house, and everything.

JOHNJOE: But you never wore one when we lived in Ireland.

JIM: Yeah, well. Obviously I wouldn't wear one in Ireland.

JOHNJOE: Is that not a bit of a hint that you shouldn't wear one at all.

Beat.

JIM: Are you alright?

JOHNJOE: What?

JIM: Is this a bad time to do this? You know with the break up/

JOHNJOE: /No it's.. I've had a bit of a full on day, but yeah we can. Has this been on like, an agenda of yours?

JIM: What do you mean?

JOHNJOE: Five o'clock—Fold the washing. Six o'clock—Piss Johnjoe off by supporting the British Army.

JIM: I don't support the British Army.

JOHNJOE: By wearing a poppy, you are supporting the British Army. End of discussion.

JIM: I don't support everything they've ever done…

JOHNJOE: Well Fuck me!

JIM: What?!

JOHNJOE: I can't believe what I'm hearing. It wasn't easy for me to teach you about what your country did on Irish soil you know? It wasn't a walk in the park, but you asked me, you made me feel like you wanted to learn and understand. But it turns out I just was pissing in the wind.

JIM: I'm not saying it's not important.

JOHNJOE: That's what it sounds like.

JIM: I'm saying.

JIM gathers himself.

I'm trying to say that listing every atrocity the British have ever committed doesn't help anyone.

Beat.

JOHNJOE: We'd also be here all night.

JIM: Right. You are right. There is no getting away from it. We are the bad guys. Cromwell, The Black and Tans. But what about the foot soldier? What about Dougie?

Stop acting like you saved me from some awful fate. The Noble Irish man who educated the poor little English boy that knew no better. It's moralistic and patronising and I'm sick of it man. Remember where you are.

Pause.

JOHNJOE lets out an over-the-top cry, mocking JIM. This goes on for longer than you'd think necessary.

JIM: Shut up.

JOHNJOE: The poor little English boy is checked on his privilege and throws a strop.

JIM: I am not throwing a strop.

JOHNJOE: Grow up, Jim.

JIM: No, you grow up. You've been shutting me down for 20 minutes.

I've been trying to enact a healthy discourse about this/

JOHNJOE: /I have never heard you use those words in your life.

JIM: Well, I just did.

JOHNJOE: Alright. I'm listening. I'm seeing through your ridiculous accent/

JIM: /You're the one with the accent!

JOHNJOE: Ah, so everyone's foreign when they're not English.

JIM: When we're in England, yes actually.

JOHNJOE: You understand how arrogant that is to think you're the centre of the world?

JIM: Aw mate, give it a rest.

JOHNJOE: What?

JIM: So no one's foreign and no one's English; I see it now.

There are no borders. Oh this is revolutionary.

We're all frolicking around in our white skirts and we meet up with the fairies every Friday, where we have a feast of organic produce. And then we go to bed under a big warm turf of grass but wait… the fairies are still here and they're tickling us. Tickle fight with the fairies. Tickle fight with the fairies—is that really the world you think we live in?

JOHNJOE: That's not exactly what I was trying to say.

JIM: There are some things that just are—and you have to stop talking in ideas and gestures, accept them and move on.

Pause.

JOHNJOE: Ypres was the first world war.

JIM: What?

JOHNJOE: The Assembly thing. Ypres was the first world war.

JIM: Yeah…

JOHNJOE: The Nazi's was World War Two. You're all mixed up.

JIM: So?

JOHNJOE: You're telling me to accept things but you're wrong about those things.
You don't even know the history that you're clinging onto.

Pause.

JIM: It's all the Germans, fuck 'em

JOHNJOE: Well, that's Xenophobic.

JIM: No actually, yeah, because I get it. They don't align themselves with what they did in the 20th century. But it still happened innit? I'm not saying they need to be chastised for their history but they ought to be reminded, like 'yeah good one mate but your Grandad was a Nazi'.

JOHNJOE: And yet when I bring up your 20th century you say I ought to forget about it?

JIM: Have I not apologised enough! Accepted enough abuse? You remember St Patricks Day 2019?

JIM exits.

7: BOO THE BRIT IS REALISM

A murmur of a crowd is heard. A pub in Dublin. The blazers/badges are not used.

A change in lighting state; Surrealism.

JOHNJOE directs this to the audience.

JOHNJOE: Alright, who's new? Who just got here? We're doing Boo the Brit. What we're doing right, is we're going to boo him. We've done it since we got up today, every hour on the hour. He's at the bar right now but when he comes in, just boo him. He knows it's a bit of craic it's fine. So just boo and when you think it's too long just keep booing. It's grand he gets it. It's our day.

JIM enters. JOHNJOE Encourages the audience to boo.

JIM: Still? You're still doing this?

Very funny, yeah. Fair play to you

JIM spots someone in the crowd.

No, yeah cause I've been buying your drinks all night so you can fuck off.

JIM exits.

JOHNJOE resumes his position in the chair.

A murmur from the crowd dies down.

8: FRIENDSHIP IS REALISM IV

JIM re-enters.

The lighting state returns to realism.

JOHNJOE: So… You didn't enjoy Boo the Brit?

JIM: No I did not enjoy boo the brit.

JOHNJOE: It was funny!

JIM: It was mean.

JOHNJOE: It was both!

JIM: Exactly. For years I've put up with everything you threw at me and accepted your version of events and now I don't have anything left that I can call my own.

JOHNJOE: All I'm saying is that you can't say that the poppy is the world wars and not the occupation of Ireland.

Pause.

JIM: Fuck the French too.

JOHNJOE: They were on your side!

JIM: 'The French' is a different thing. I just don't like the French.

JOHNJOE: I get it, you're being funny and reductive, but if we're having a serious conversation, then we're having a serious conversation.

JIM: I'm allowed to say some things.

JOHNJOE: No one is saying that you can't.

JIM: Yes they are.

JOHNJOE: Who?

Beat.

Who is stopping you from saying anything, Jim?

JIM: You know who.

JOHNJOE: If you say what I think you're about to say/

JIM: /Woke Mob.

JOHNJOE: Woke Mob are not coming for you hating the French!

Beat.

JIM: You're saying I'm allowed to hate the French.

JOHNJOE: Of course.

JIM: I thought it was xenophobic?

JOHNJOE: Oh no, it's fine when it's the French

Pause.

An excitable realisation hits JIM.

JIM: They look down on everyone!

JOHNJOE: They're so up their own arses!

JIM: Thank you!

JOHNJOE: Everyone hates the French.

JIM: You're saying this whole time I hated the French, you hated them too.

JOHNJOE: Yeah.

JIM: Woah.

JOHNJOE: The enemy of my enemy.

BOTH: Is my friend!

JIM: Fuck the French!

JOHNJOE: Fuck 'em!

BOTH laugh.

Pause.

JOHNJOE: I'm happy you were in, man. It's good to see you. It's been a long month.

Pause.

JIM Ponders. A gear shift.

JIM: The Irish don't hate the French the way the English hate the French.

JOHNJOE: Jim!

JIM: We hate the French.

JOHNJOE: The whole world hates the French, Jim.

JIM: Not in the way that we do, it's an English thing to hate the French so much.

JOHNJOE: Jesus you're obsessed with claiming things aren't you, can't help yourself.

JIM: You've got to be honest—we hate people really well.

JOHNJOE: No denying that.

JIM: Especially the French.

JOHNJOE: Why? Because they're better than you?

JIM: Careful now.

JOHNJOE: Because they actually know how to make good cheese?

JIM: Red Leicester over Brie every day of the week/

JOHNJOE: Because they know how to revolt.

JIM: Maybe, yeah. They do stand up for themselves when they're trodden on.

9: CORPORATE SURREALISM

A change in lighting state; Surrealism.

The actors put on their Poppy blazers once more. JOHNJOE replaces the 'POPPY' badge with 'NOT A POPPY' badge. JIM's blazer has a 'POPPY' badge.

Johnjoe plays BOSS, Jim plays EMPLOYEE.

BOSS: Please come in.

BOSS directs EMPLOYEE to seat centre stage facing out to the audience.

BOSS: Thank you for seeing me.

EMPLOYEE: No danger, no stress.

BOSS: I want you to look out there and tell me what you see.

EMPLOYEE: Uhhh…

BOSS: Don't be shy. There are no wrong answers.

EMPLOYEE:… The Office…?

BOSS: Wrong. You know what I see? A beautiful hive of little worker bees all striving towards the same goal; making that delicious honey.

EMPLOYEE: IT Support?

BOSS: Which is our Honey. As you can see, we're a company that has gone from strength to strength in our first six months, and you know our slogan here, do it with me now;

Both say the slogan, BOSS enthusiastically, EMPLOYEE reluctantly.

BOTH: Cash Money Baby!

BOSS: Yes, Very good! Which has resulted in us recruiting a bigger team than we had ever forecasted at this stage.

EMPLOYEE: Are you letting me go? Because I really was sick last week.

BOSS: We know.

EMPLOYEE: I know the Oasis gig was on, but I wasn't there.

BOSS: We trust you.

EMPLOYEE: My insta was hacked,

BOSS: OK.

EMPLOYEE: I was not on ketamine at Oasis when I should have been at a staff training day.

BOSS: What I'm trying to say is that the office has hired a large breadth of people who have views that may contrast with yours—

EMPLOYEE:—Oh. Yeah of course.

BOSS: And a formal complaint has been lodged against you and your etiquette.

EMPLOYEE: I'm sorry, what?

BOSS: We're here to help you learn and grow as an individual that aligns with our values as a company.

EMPLOYEE: How am I not aligning with our values? I was here from the start. I am the values.

BOSS: That's not the case here.

EMPLOYEE: Was this about Rohan the other day?

BOSS: Now we're not going to get into specifics/

EMPLOYEE: For the last time I didn't say pooowee curry/

BOSS: I'm sorry, what?/

EMPLOYEE: /I said: yipee curry, again for the fourth day in a row.

BOSS: Now this is a whole other thing that I was not aware of.

EMPLOYEE: Then what is this about?

BOSS: We all have our political allegiances, but we try to not make them clear in the office.

EMPLOYEE: What allegiances?

BOSS: Certain emblems or pins, that don't align with what we represent as a company.

EMPLOYEE: Is this seriously what I think it's about?

BOSS: I think you know.

EMPLOYEE: Who lodged this complaint?

JOHNJOE: I'm not at liberty to disclaim.

EMPLOYEE: Who was it?! Because I'd like to have a conversation with them.

BOSS: They have come to me in confidence.

EMPLOYEE: Shut up, with this fake scenario, I know it's you.

BOSS: I don't know what you're/

EMPLOYEE: /I'm serious, let's have a discussion like actual people.

Pause.

BOSS: Fine, yes it was me—

EMPLOYEE: So did you want to ask me why I wear one or are you just going to assume.

BOSS: That's not my concern.

EMPLOYEE: That friends of mine have killed themselves serving for this country, is that not of your concern?

BOSS: There's really no need.

EMPLOYEE: And this charity, this thing on my chest is how I remember them? Have you ever thought about that?

BOSS: You needn't display that trauma in the office.

EMPLOYEE: I'm just giving a pound to the people who were there for his wife when he died.

BOSS: Don't manipulate me.

EMPLOYEE: Why is saying how I feel manipulative?

BOSS: You know what you're doing.

EMPLOYEE: Why do you feel the need to keep this corporate setting to do it?

BOSS: We have a multi-cultural office.

EMPLOYEE: And?

BOSS: I'm not the only one who feels this.

EMPLOYEE: Have you even gone through HR?

BOSS: Don't have to. I know my staff and I know how this turns out if you try to resist.

EMPLOYEE: Resist what?

Are you going to wrestle it off me?

BOSS: Of course not.

EMPLOYEE: Then it will stay on. Thank you very much. Unless you want to go through HR and do it properly, you weasel, because I think I know what side they'd be on.

BOSS: I'm not sure they'd be as supportive as you might think.

Pause.

EMPLOYEE exhales, considers.

BOSS: Seems like a simple decision to me.

Pause.

BOSS: Do you need me to take it off? Will that help?

BOSS walks towards EMPLOYEE.

EMPLOYEE: Do not come a step closer to me.

BOSS: Make it simple. For the good of the Hive.

EMPLOYEE takes off his 'POPPY' badge

EMPLOYEE: Fine. Fine. There you go. Are you happy? Can I go now?

Beat.

A deep underscore to illicit dread is heard

EMPLOYEE: What? What are you looking at me all menacing for?

BOSS: Now dance.

EMPLOYEE: What?

BOSS puts on a tri-colour balaclava and pulls out a gun.

BOSS: Dance for me, boy.

Irish Trad music starts and BOSS shoots a blank at EMPLOYEE's feet.

BOSS: I SAID DANCE, BRIT!

EMPLOYEE dances out of fear.

BOSS sits and strokes his gun and laughs maniacally. A manic lighting state.

10: FRIENDSHIP IS REALISM V

Snap back to Realism.

The performers put their blazers back on the mannequins.

A change in lighting state.

JOHNJOE: What the hell was that?

JIM: What?

JOHNJOE: You know what! You almost had a point. You were so close and you ruined it with that mad shit at the end!

JIM: What? That could happen!

JOHNJOE pauses.

JOHNJOE: Jim, You actually think that could happen?

Pause.

JIM: Maybe. I dunno!
It's not as far from the truth as you might think.

JOHNJOE: Are you really afraid of that? You think that's what I want?

JIM: Most veterans are good people.

JOHNJOE: Sure.

JIM: I don't think they should be chastised for that just because they're taken advantage of, by their governments.

JOHNJOE: I get it.

JIM: No you don't.

JOHNJOE: I do.

Pause. JOHNJOE considers.

My Great Grandad Eddie fought in World War One.

JIM: For the Brits?

JOHNJOE: No, for the fucking Japanese, who do you think?

JIM: I dunno. It's just hard to imagine someone so close to you fighting for us.

JOHNJOE: Yeah. When I first heard that I didn't really know what to think. Shook me a bit.

JIM: So, you're ashamed of him or something? Doesn't fit with your perfect little Irish identity?

JOHNJOE: No.

JIM: And now you're upset with me for wanting to wear something that remembers him?

JOHNJOE: It's not that simple, Jim, especially since when he came back he housed Irish revolutionaries who were fighting against the Brits.

JIM: So what side was he on?

JOHNJOE: I don't really know. I mean tonnes of Irish nationalists who fought in the war were encouraged to sign up by Irish political leaders. The British government promised them a parliament in Dublin once the war was over, but that obviously didn't happen/

JIM: /Well the poppy remembers them too then! Your countrymen who were misled and sent to their deaths, just like mine were.

JOHNJOE: Sure. But now,they've taken this symbol and warped it to create this image of the Empire that's false. They tell you that these young men, your 'heroes' are what the Empire was and still is. And only that. They want you to ignore the rest of its blood soaked legacy. A legacy that persists even today.

JIM: Every country has a history they're not proud of. Including yours.

JOHNJOE: But I don't think you get to ignore it.

Jim, I get it. It's complex and ugly and sad and it hurts.

But you don't get to remember the time you were heroes and forget all the times you were villains.

JIM: The poppy does good. It supports families that have lost loved ones, homelessness, PTSD.

JOHNJOE: Right yeah, and if Benjamin Netanyahu started doing community work on the weekends, would you say he's a great lad and we should support him too??

JIM: That's ridiculous! You can't say every soldier is a war criminal. Most of them are good men/

JOHNJOE: /The good it does doesn't cancel out the bad it represents too. The bad that you want us to forget about. After that display, I don't think you have a clue what you're saying or where you stand

JIM: I know that stuff like that has happened. It is happening.

JOHNJOE: There's like this colonial fear that's been baked into you; that if people who used to be beneath you get a semblance of power over you, they'll treat you the same way that you treated them.

JIM: I never treated you or anyone like that and I never would.

JOHNJOE: I don't know whether you even know you do it. But deep down it's like you still think that you in some way own us.

JIM: How do we act like we own you?

JOHNJOE: Think of any Irish celebrity, actor or band, the moment they get famous enough, the British media claims em;

'British Actor Cillian Murphy nominated for an Oscar.'

'Amazing new British band, Fontaines DC win the Mercury Prize.' I don't think there's an Irish celebrity you could name that hasn't been claimed as British

Beat.

JIM: ... Jedward... Jedward!

JOHNJOE: Alright… K, no they haven't been I guess… But you can have them, we'll gladly donate them to you. Them and Conor McGregor. He's definitely a Brit now too.

JIM: Ugh no, we do not want him.

JOHNJOE: Jesus, stop the presses, the Brits turn down the possibility of claiming an Irish person! It's a miracle!

JIM: Johnjoe/

JOHNJOE: /it's not even just us! Every time Andy Murray won at Wimbledon, he was British, the second he loses, he's Scottish again.

JIM: Well to be fair they are still part of/

JOHNJOE: /Or any English football player of colour; when they're doing well 'ah they're great English lads aren't they' but if they miss a penalty it's 'Go back to your own country'.

JIM: What's that got to do with anything?

JOHNJOE: Membership of your 'Empire' seems to be very much based on how useful you're deemed to be at any given moment. We want no part of it and yet you still try to suck us in, still try to force it on us.

JIM: Look mate. You live over here, you're gonna see poppies. No ones forcing you to wear one

JOHNJOE: What about any Irish person on any talk show on the BBC around November?

You think they want to wear a poppy? Or do you think that they're made to, like everyone else who comes near a camera over here around this time.

JIM: Oh, you think they're getting them pinned on by force?

11. FAME IS SURREALISM

The lighting state returns to realism.

The actors put on their poppy blazers once more. JIM with POPPY. JOHNJOE with 'NOT A POPPY'

JIM plays PRODUCER. JOHNJOE plays CELEB.

PRODUCER: And this is our green room, we have air conditioning set at 19 degrees, as requested, we have blue tulips as opposed to red for feng shui and an oat chai latte for you here.

PRODUCER hands JOHNJOE a coffee.

We are just thrilled to have you on, dude.

CELEB: I'm thrilled to be here.

PRODUCER: Fantastic, love it. We know it's not the nicest of places to get to but the hire of this place is dirt cheap for the taxpayer and I just Uber in and Uber out every day, don't even pop out for lunch. Here's a QR code for free Pret, if you go downstairs past the yoga studio, sling a left, there's a room that says 'Prayer Room' but really it's a secret Pret. So cool dude. Do you do TikTok?

CELEB: TikTok? No. Oh, well I did do this thing with my niece the other week where we kind of… I don't really know what we did but it made her happy so I guess sometimes I Tik-tok.

PRODUCER: 'I Tik Tok'. Your accent is brilliant. Never heard it used as a verb before.

That's great. You are just great!

CELEB: Thanks.

PRODUCER: So we just need a bit of content for socials so fans of yours can tune in and know what to expect this weekend. Is that all OK, dude?

CELEB: Sure.

PRODUCER: Are you mic'd up, dude? Can I check quickly?

CELEB: Sure, whatever you need to. God you're right up in there.

PRODUCER: Any holibobs coming up?

CELEB: Oh yes, actually. I've got this, then The One Show tomorrow and after that I'm headed to Turkey.

PRODUCER: Oh lovely. Getting your hair done?

CELEB: What? No.

PRODUCER: Teeth?

CELEB: No.

PRODUCER: Had Gosling in here the other week, went Turkey had the lot, looks a mess. Be careful out there, dude.

CELEB: I'm not going there for/

PRODUCER: /Don't want you losing that Irish charm.

CELEB: Right.

PRODUCER: Very in right now.

CELEB: Thank you?

PRODUCER: And if you can just pop this on for me that'd be fantastic.

PRODUCER holds out something that represents a poppy.

CELEB: Ah. No. Erm. No thank you.

PRODUCER: Works with your eyes brilliantly.

CELEB: Even so.

PRODUCER: It'll really pop.

CELEB: No it won't because I won't be wearing one.

JOHNJOE gestures towards the poppy.

Beat.

PRODUCER: You don't want to wear the poppy?

CELEB: No

PRODUCER: Not even a little one?

PRODUCER reaches into the pocket of his blazer and pulls out a smaller version of the 'Poppy' pin.

CELEB: No, as I've said—just not going to wear one at all.

PRODUCER: ... But... Why not...?

CELEB: Just not comfortable with what it represents really.

PRODUCER: The war effort? I know you guys were neutral or whatever but...

CELEB: More have an issue with the support for the British Military.

PRODUCER: I see...

CELEB: So I wouldn't be comfortable wearing that. I'm sure you can understand

PRODUCER: ...Well, actually

CELEB: Yes?

PRODUCER: You kind of *have* to wear one.

CELEB: Have to?

PRODUCER: Yeah, everyone on the show does around this time —it's for the best

CELEB: In what way?

PRODUCER: I mean we get a lot of complaints from the programming office if someone is seen not to be remembering our heroes and you... I mean, the backlash online is always quite... intense.

CELEB: I think I'll be OK.

PRODUCER: If you say so! Just you know… as someone trying to make a comeback in their career… it may not be the best move… just saying

CELEB: Are you threatening me?

PRODUCER: No! No, course not, wouldn't dream of it, just some advice!

CELEB: Sure.

PRODUCER: The edit may not be kind to you if you refuse to wear it.

CELEB: Excuse me?

PRODUCER: Yeah, stuff like that has happened before—guys have come in and chatted away for hours and then the edit comes back and it's like they were never even there. Magic of TV; so cool, dude.

CELEB: This is ridiculous, you can't police what I wear.

PRODUCER: Course we can, thank God you're not trying to wear a Palestine pin now.

(laughs) Don't even get me started on that whole fiasco.

CELEB: Well actually…

PRODUCER: Look, dude, can you just play ball for us please, we're in a hurry.

CELEB: Play ball? Look can I speak to him, he is Irish/

PRODUCER grabs his hand and pins him to the floor.

JOHNJOE yelps.

PRODUCER speaks in a tone that depicts hell. Tech elements should enhance this.

PRODUCER: You will submit to the almighty beast that is Graham Norton and you will wear a Poppy in November on BBC prime time to respect our heroes. For they are all heroes. They are all infallible and yet they fell, for you, for this and you will thank them. Blasted be your Irishness, you will thank them by wearing this paper flower or you shall feel the wrath of the devil himself! Dude!

JOHNJOE stumbles back across the floor clutching his elbow.

12: FALLING OUT IS REALISM

Snap back to; Realism

BOTH take off their blazers and return them to the mannequins.

JIM: Well, that's what you're saying, isn't it? I'm evil, I'm the Devil.

JOHNJOE: I mean not you, that wasn't supposed to be you. You can't just throw me to the floor like that.

JIM: I thought it was a pretty cool character choice.

JOHNJOE: I hit my elbow.

JIM: I didn't know you'd go down.

JOHNJOE: You hurt me.

JIM: Let me look.

JOHNJOE: You can't just man handle me like that with no warning.

JIM: I know.

There's no mark. You're fine.

Pause.

JOHNJOE: This is exactly it—whenever I stand up for my Irishness I get hurt.

JIM: If a fella has to wear a poppy to sell a film then so be it. There are worse evils.

JOHNJOE: But they don't have a choice.

JIM: I'm finding it very hard to sympathise with a bunch of millionaires.

JOHNJOE: It makes no difference—it's the principle of an Englishman forcing an Irishman to do something against his will.

JIM: You know what you're right. I hope they're OK and not crying themselves to sleep at night in their three bed flat on Hampstead Heath.

JOHNJOE: Stuff like that has happened to me too.

JIM: Like what?

JOHNJOE: A tutor in drama school brought up my Irishness on multiple occasions.

Used it in directing notes for other people. Told me to act the "classic Irish Idiot" or told people to treat me like I was "Bog Irish" like my nationality is a synonym for stupidity.

JIM: Johnjoe/

JOHNJOE: /Do you think an Irish Tutor would have said something like that to me?

JIM: Oh, was drama school tough for you? Did Brecht take its toll?

JOHNJOE: See! Here it is! You want to talk about identity and nationality until I talk about mine and you have to hear something that you don't like.

JIM: Because I'm constantly having to justify my Englishness.

JOHNJOE: Since when?

JIM: Since forever.

JOHNJOE: Then why is all this coming out now? Why now?

JIM: I think it's about time that I picked a side. Know my principles and live by them.

Fall into the arms of my country.

Beat.

JOHNJOE: You're talking like you're this soldier at war. Looking for someone to be your enemy. Who are you fighting, Jim?

Is it me?

You're turning into the type of person we used to laugh at.

JIM: That you used to laugh at. I have to hide that I'm proud to be English in my own country, while you just get to flaunt your Irishness and wear this victimhood like a badge of honour.

JOHNJOE: And why should I not wear it? My people have come back from the brink from suffering inflicted by your ancestors.

JIM: Not mine ,mate. My ancestors were starving in East London at the same time yours were in Ireland.

JOHNJOE: Did yours survive a famine? A man-made famine. A British-made famine?

JIM: Ugh, I'm so sick of this constant victim mentality.

JOHNJOE: Victim mentality? Your country? Can you hear yourself right now?

JIM: It is my country. You love this country, I know you do. That accent is practically the reason Georgia went out with you in the first place!

JOHNJOE: I love living over here. The people I've met, sure.

But I don't love this country. I don't feel held by this country.

Not in the way I feel held by my home. By Ireland.

It's not easy for me over here. I'm constantly on edge. It's exhausting.

I walk down streets lined with Union Jacks. I meet people on nights out who make ignorant comments or jokes about the Irish.

I've had to grow used to that feeling. Being forced to make that decision; take issue with it or let it slide. Let it eat away at me. I lose either way, reduced to the 'fun Irish guy' or the 'Paddy who can't take a joke'.

But I can deal with that. I'm going to meet pricks like that, course I am. But you?

Now this is happening right now in front of me, with you.

And the onus is on me again. To accept this, you, whatever you're becoming or take issue with it. Now you're the one asking me to choose to either say something or shrink into myself.

JIM: Maybe you should.

JOHNJOE: Maybe I should—what?

JIM: When we were in Dublin. I felt small. And I told myself that that was OK because it was yours and I was lucky to be there with you. But now I'm back where I grew up and I still feel small.

JOHNJOE: How has that got anything to do with me?

JIM: You're still big. You're still this character that people love to be around and I'm your mate again. How have I come back to my country and still I'm a plus one? I'm still not able to be proud of where I'm from. I still need to hide parts of myself away when I'm with you.

JOHNJOE: You didn't have to be that way in Ireland.

JIM: Oh yeah, cause me talking about loving England and wearing a poppy would have gone down real smooth over in Dublin??

JOHNJOE: I'm not saying that, but yeah you could have, if that's what you actually wanted to be. You not being brave enough to stand up for yourself and what you say you believe in, isn't my fault.

JIM: Well, now I am. I do believe in this.

JOHNJOE: Funny though isn't it? That this only comes out when you're back in "your" country surrounded by people that sound like you and think like you. You're not pissed off at me cause I'm proud of where I'm from, you're pissed off that you didn't have the conviction to defend your own pride in your country when it was hard. And now that you feel comfortable again you want me to get back in my box and be grateful? You feign care and love for this country over things that are actually happening to us.

JIM: Us?

JOHNJOE: I'm just glad we're talking.

We don't talk anymore, Jim. It's been weeks.

It's like you're always going somewhere with someone else.

JIM: You're one to talk, you're practically out every night of the week.

JOHNJOE: And I invite you to those things.

JIM: I don't want to go to things with other people

JOHNJOE: How is that on me?

JIM: Where I'm taken the piss out of/

JOHNJOE: /Tonight's the first night I've seen you in weeks and you want to talk about poppies? Do you know how ridiculous that is? After the month I've had.

Pause.

JIM: Look, I'm sorry about your break up but…

JOHNJOE: Go on.

JIM: This is why she broke up with you.

JOHNJOE: I'm sorry?

JIM: If you don't want to hear it/

JOHNJOE: There are plenty of reasons why we broke up, actually you don't have any of the information.

JIM: I reckon I can put two and two together.

JOHNJOE: What the fuck is that supposed to mean?

JIM: How you spoke to her and me wasn't too different. I was there that night you made her cry. And I know that wasn't the only time. You take your shame and fear of losing who you are—your Irishness. It came out against her the same way it's always come out against me. You mask your feelings. You demean.

You belittle. For some reason you're comfortable doing that to those you love. I think you ought to look into that.

JOHNJOE: Don't therapise me.

JIM: Just trying to help.

JOHNJOE: Are you?

JIM: If you were open to discussion the way that I am then she wouldn't have left you.

JOHNJOE: Hold on… have you spoken to her?

JIM: We met up for a coffee for a chat a couple of weeks ago, yeah.

JOHNJOE: Are you serious?

JIM: She was wondering how you were doing/

JOHNJOE: /How would you know how I'm doing?

JIM: Are you really upset that I spoke to her? We're friends too/

JOHNJOE: /You haven't even spoken to me!

Do you want to hear why we broke up? If you're so invested/

JIM: Listen mate/

JOHNJOE: /I couldn't organise a date without having a panic attack.

I kept her from my family in case they said something about her being English. I chose making strangers laugh over a night in with her.

I couldn't afford to take her out for dinner and then I made it her problem for expecting that from me.

I overslept and was three hours late to meeting her for coffee and she had to sit there waiting.

And you know what? You're right. I took out my anger and shame on her instead of the prick who said something to me.

I turned my haven of a relationship into a political, ugly arena and I lost someone who I truly loved because of it.

Happy now?

JIM: /I didn't even ask.

JOHNJOE: Exactly, you never asked me. But you intruded. You made time for her and you never checked in on me. I needed you and you haven't been here for me.

At all.

JIM: I didn't want to have this conversation today.

JOHNJOE: But here we are. We're having it. Some new hollow, angry part of you did want this.

JIM: Who I am is not hollow.

JOHNJOE: You've got no personality of your own other than being jealous of me.

JIM: That's out of order, Johnjoe.

JOHNJOE: You abandoned me.

JIM: A break up is difficult/

JOHNJOE: /I'm not even talking about the break up.

We used to actually be friends, we used to tell each other everything.

I was so excited when I saw you tonight. All I wanted to do was have a cup of tea with you. But apparently we can't even do that anymore. Which is fine, maybe. If I tell myself that people grow apart. It hurts me but it happens. But to rub salt into my wounds. You've come back with these big new principles and ideas that completely shut me out. Completely invalidate me and my experience. I want you to tell me how you feel. Of course I do. But you're pulling away from me, Jim. Why?

Pause.

Because I don't agree with you on wearing a fucking poppy? You can't expect me to agree with you on this?

JIM: I expect you not to belittle who I am.

JOHNJOE: But you're so much more than this. We're so much more than this.

Do I mean that little to you? Am I just your 'Irish friend'? Because you're my best friend, man.

JIM: Johnjoe, there's no need to get emoti/

JOHNJOE: /There is. Actually there is.

JIM: I brought this all about in a measured manner/

JOHNJOE: /Yeah you've been very diplomatic.

JIM: You bring this anger out of me.

JOHNJOE: It's in your blood. With your nationalism comes this belief that your feelings are more valid than mine.

JIM: No matter how nicely I'm trying to put something, it comes back to that.

JOHNJOE: All I need to hear from you is that I'm valid.

JIM: I always communicate in a healthy way.

JOHNJOE: Am I valid? Tell me I'm valid.

JIM: It's always a shouting match with you somehow. I try to be calm/

JOHNJOE: /Congratulations on your polite manner. Your wonderful decorum and British stiff upper lip.

JIM: That's my identity, I'm not apologising for it anymore.

JOHNJOE: Your identity is nothing more than looking down on those you colonised and tip toeing around your cold-hearted Dads.

JIM: Because the Irish are so open and warm aren't you? Like you're not an island of botched abortions and alcoholics.

13: MIDDLE OF THE PLAY

A change in lighting state—The same state that is used in 'Beginning of the Play' and 'End of the Play'. The performers address the audience directly. The blazers/badges are not used.

JOHNJOE: I can't believe you just said that.

JIM: I can't believe I just said that.

JOHNJOE: Do you think that?

JIM: I'd like to think I don't think that.

JOHNJOE: I don't even know what we're talking about anymore.

BOTH: This is meant to be about poppies.

JIM: It is about poppies.

JOHNJOE: That upset me. I'm allowed to be upset by that.

JIM: It's just a poppy.

JOHNJOE: It's all mixed up.

JIM: It's about poppies.

JOHNJOE: In everything else.

JIM: It's just a poppy, let me have a poppy.

JOHNJOE: I'm all mixed up, you were meant to be there for me.

JIM: You're meant to understand my point of view.

JOHNJOE: It's about poppies.

JIM: It's about poppies.

JOHNJOE: You hurt me.

JIM: It's about poppies.

JOHNJOE: You can't even see that you're hurting me.

JIM: It's about poppies.

JOHNJOE: How much do you need this?

JIM: It's about poppies.

JOHNJOE: You need this more than you need me?

JIM: It's about poppies.

JOHNJOE: You see that you're hurting me.

JIM: It's about poppies.

JOHNJOE: Fine. It's about poppies.

JIM: It's about poppies.

JOHNJOE: Congratulations. It's about poppies.

BOTH: It's about poppies.

JIM: I'm sorry.

JOHNJOE: It's fine. It's about poppies.

JIM: I'm sorry, I didn't mean that, I didn't mean half of it.

JOHNJOE: It's about poppies now.

JIM: But the half I did mean I really meant.

JOHNJOE: It's about poppies.

JIM: It's just I had this one thing.

JOHNJOE: It's about poppies.

JIM: And I want this one thing. Can you not let me have this one thing?

JOHNJOE: It's about poppies.

BOTH: It's about poppies.

14: CRITIQUE IS SURREALISM

A change in lighting state; Surrealism.

Performers put on the blazers.

JIM plays VOICE 1. JOHNJOE plays VOICE 2

VOICE 1: It feels like they've pulled back.

BOTH: Poppies.

VOICE 2: I came here to see some political theatre.

BOTH: Poppies.

VOICE 1: They're not committing to anything.

BOTH: Poppies.

VOICE 2: They haven't got the balls to make it about poppies.

BOTH: Poppies.

VOICE 1: Is it a men's mental health play all of a sudden?

BOTH: Poppies.

VOICE 2: I've had it up to here with men's mental health.

BOTH: Poppies.

VOICE 1: Even if it is that, then it's underbaked.

BOTH: Poppies.

VOICE 2: Is it about his break up or something?

BOTH: Poppies.

VOICE 1: Should I wear one or not?

BOTH: Poppies.

VOICE 2: Hello? Should I wear a poppy or not, please?

BOTH: Poppies.

VOICE 1: Make a statement. Say something. Take a stance.

BOTH: It's about poppies.

VOICE 2: Are your generation so scared of saying how you feel?

BOTH: It's about poppies.

VOICE 1: You think you're so smart.

BOTH: Poppies.

VOICE 2: That if you say...

BOTH: It's about Poppies.

VOICE 1: ... over and over again the audience will realise it's not about poppies.

Beat.

BOTH: It's about poppies.

Beat. A change in tone.

BOTH: Oh! It's about poppies!

BOTH: You should have said!

VOICE 1: Shall we do it how they ought to?

VOICE 2: Sounds good to me.

VOICE 1: On your mark.

VOICE 2: Get set.

BOTH: Go.

VOICE 1: Hello!

VOICE 2: Hello!

VOICE 1: I'm English.

VOICE 2: I'm Irish.

BOTH: Grrrrrr.

VOICE 1: I want to wear a poppy.

VOICE 2: You shouldn't wear a poppy.

VOICE 1: You should wear a poppy.

VOICE 2: You have your points.

VOICE 1: You have yours.

VOICE 2: We don't agree.

VOICE 1: We never will.

VOICE 2: That's the play done.

VOICE 1: Four lines.

VOICE 2: 10 words each.

VOICE 1: Finito.

VOICE 2: End of play.

VOICE 1: Could have saved you the ticket price. Cup of tea?

VOICE 2: Yes please.

VOICE 1: Irish tea or bad tea?

VOICE 2: Haha. He gets it, See?

VOICE 1: We're friends still! See?

VOICE 2: We live in the grey area in between, you see?

VOICE 1: We all do!

BOTH: That's life.

BOTH: Well then, let's move on.

15: DOUGIE TELLEY IS REALISM (?)

Fade to low light/blackout.

The interview with Dougie Telley is projected—a continuation of what was seen before. As it starts JIM breaks out of the stylised segment we were just in.

Performers remove their blazers and replace them on the mannequins.

JIM: No. Turn it off.

JOHNJOE: What?

JIM: How did you get this? Turn it off.

JOHNJOE: Why are you blaming me? I didn't do anything.

JIM: Cian *(Tech Operator's name)*, turn it off. This wasn't part of the video.

JOHNJOE: Everything has been on your terms.

JIM: Cian *(/Tech Operator's name)* turn the VT off.

JOHNJOE: You're in charge.

JIM: There has been no/

JOHNJOE: /You write the curriculum.

JIM: I don't do anything.
This is different, Dougie Telley is different.

JOHNJOE: To what you think he is.

The Dougie Telley interview continues with the quote

"WE SAILED THE SEVEN SEA'S AND WE KILLED THEM ALL"

JIM: Cian *(Tech Operator's name)* turn it off! Do not touch our veterans.

JOHNJOE: Not ours. Yours.

JIM: Fine. Do not touch my veterans. Do not touch men like me.

JOHNJOE: Just because you want him to be like you doesn't make him like you.

JIM: He's an old man!

JOHNJOE: When he dies, with him goes this image of Britain in your head.

JIM: How can you do this?

JOHNJOE: When your veterans are just soldiers who shot Irish children in the back, where do you go from there?

JIM: How dare you use him to push your agenda.

JOHNJOE: That's what you've been doing this whole time.

JIM: He hardly even knows what's going on.

JOHNJOE: He remembers what he did.

JIM: Save the world as we know it?

JOHNJOE: Get away with murder under the guise of a Union Jack.

JIM: If it weren't for people like him you'd be speaking German.

JOHNJOE: If it weren't for people like him I'd be speaking Irish.

16: IRISH IS REALISM

Flicker/Change in lighting state. The shift between these states is immediate.

JOHNJOE becomes SEÁNSEO, JIM becomes SÉAMAS. The blazers/badges are not used. A translation of the Irish is projected on the screen behind SEÁNSEO and SÉAMAS.

SEÁNSEO: Féach ort féin. Tá tú comh feargach. Caithfidh tú stop a chur le seo.

[Look at yourself. You're so angry. You have to put a stop to this]

SÉAMAS: Níl mé ábalta. Tá seo ag teastáil uaim. Tá rud éigin mícheart, rud éigin caillte Agam.

[I'm not able to. I need this. Something is wrong, I've lost something.]

SEÁNSEO: Féach orm. Féach orm.

[Look at me. Look at me.]

Fan socair agus fan liom. Táim tuirseach de bheith ag argóint leat, nil seo cé a bhfuil muid.

[Stay calm and stay with me. I'm tired of arguing with you, this isn't who we are.]

SÉAMAS: Tá sé. Tá sé anois.

[It is. It is now.]

17: FALLING OUT IS REALISM AGAIN

Flicker/Change in lighting state. Returns to Realism.

JIM: You don't get to do that.

JOHNJOE: This whole time you've been in control, I've been an Irish device for you to get your point across.

JIM: What point?

JOHNJOE: To push this idea of Britain that doesn't exist.

JIM: It could though if people like me were able to talk about it.

JOHNJOE: You want people to leave thinking that it is sad that you can't be proud to be British when even the man you idolise was a cunt.

JIM: And the men you idolise were all saints weren't they? Ireland has no black marks on their history at all.

JOHNJOE: They're not on video bragging about it.

JIM: He's a real man who made a real sacrifice

JOHNJOE: For a regime/

JIM: You never listen to what I'm actually trying to say.
This is important to me.

JOHNJOE: I know, Jim, but since when did it become all you care about?

JIM: Because you've treated me like shit for too long. And you brag about being held by your country but mock me for wanting the same thing.

JOHNJOE: And I'm sorry I make you feel like that but/

JIM: Then change.
If you're sorry. Try it with me.

They pause. They slow down.

JOHNJOE: Try what?

JIM: Your Great Grandad was in the British Army right?

JOHNJOE: Before Irish Independence/

JIM: Exactly. So just. You pretend you're him and I'll pretend I'm my Great Grandad.

JOHNJOE: What is this going to achieve, Jim?

JIM: Just try something for me. Please. For once see my side of things.

JOHNJOE: After what you said/

JIM: I know, I know. I'm sorry. Please.

You're right. I'm sorry.

But I need this.

Just forget yourself for one minute. Please do this for me.

JOHNJOE: Jim/

JIM: /I'm my Great Grandad. You're yours—and we're at Ypres. OK?

JIM starts moving the boxes from their positions to represent the graves he describes.

JOHNJOE: This is stupid/

JIM: /And we're looking at all the graves, thousands of graves of our fellow soldiers—our mates, all dead.

All killed, all taken far too young.

JOHNJOE: Why do you want to do this?

JIM: Because all we've done all night is talk.

We talk bollocks upon bollocks without doing anything. We discuss without any movement, without any growth, without any conclusion.

With you not listening to how I feel once. Not once have you ever listened to me. Acknowledged me. That it might be the tiniest bit sad that I don't get to celebrate who I am in the same way that you do. Everything between us has always been on your terms. Who I am, my ideas have always bounced against the wall of... you. Your identity and your opinions. So strong. So assured.

So listen to me. Let me have this. Let me try and get my point across. Please. Because I can't keep hitting it against this wall that you put up. It's tiring.

I'm tired. Please.

JOHNJOE: Fine.

JIM: Yeah?

JOHNJOE: Yeah. Fine. I'll listen. Whatever you need.

18: YPRES

BOTH put on the blazers from the mannequins. Both have 'POPPY' attached to it.

JIM as GREAT GRANDAD JOSEPH. JOHNJOE as GREAT GRANDAD EDDIE.

A moment of contemplation.

JOSEPH: Beautiful day.

EDDIE: I don't have a script.

JOSEPH: Improvise! You're an actor aren't you?

EDDIE: Alright.

JOSEPH: Beautiful day, isn't it?

EDDIE : Quite.

JOSEPH: It's good to see you.

EDDIE: It's good to see you too.

JOSEPH: I haven't seen you since...

EDDIE: ...The war. That big, fucking... war.

JIM shoots JOHNJOE a sharp look of anger.

He regathers himself.

JOSEPH: May I ask a bit of a strange question?

EDDIE: Go ahead.

JOSEPH: May I hold your hand?

EDDIE: Oh.

JOSEPH: I know it's peculiar. Old chap. It's just that you're the only one who really understands what we've been through. If there was a way to have this vindicated, physically that is. Even if just for a fleeting moment. I'd be ever so grateful.

EDDIE: I can't.

JOSEPH: I understand.

EDDIE: It's not that I don't want to.

JOSEPH: No, sir I get it.

EDDIE: It's just the side you're standing on.

JOSEPH: Right.

EDDIE: I don't have a hand.

JIM: Excuse me?

JOHNJOE: You'd have known this if/

JIM: Are you taking the piss?

JOHNJOE: What?

19: HAND

Lighting snaps back to Realism.

JIM takes his blazer off, JOHNJOE does the same.

BOTH return them to their mannequins.

JIM: You can't even do one thing for me without mocking me!

JOHNJOE: I'm serious he/

JIM: /You've got that little respect for me?

JOHNJOE: You asked me to be my Great Grandad—he didn't have a hand.

JIM: I let you have your monologues about Ireland.

JOHNJOE: Let me?

JIM: I'm done. I'm so done.

JOHNJOE: Jim, he didn't have a hand.

JIM: You could've left that out!

JOHNJOE: You asked to hold my hand!

JIM: It wasn't about the hand holding it was about the gesture—

JOHNJOE: —of hand holding and he didn't have a hand!

JIM: You couldn't even play it once how I wanted it. You couldn't let me have this one thing.

JOHNJOE: No I couldn't because/

JIM: /When?

JOHNJOE: What?

JIM: When did your Grandad lose his hand?

JOHNJOE: I don't know—in his fifties.

JIM: Then why are you bringing it up in my Ypres story?

JOHNJOE: I thought they were old men.

JIM: No, they were young men, visiting their dead friends' graves in the ten year anniversary of when the armistice was called.

Pause.

JOHNJOE: How the fuck was I meant to know that?

JIM: It was obvious.

JOHNJOE: It was not obvious!

JOHNJOE turns to the audience.

JOHNJOE: Was that obvious to you?

Hopefully someone in the audience laughs at this point.

JIM: *(Towards the audience)* What are you laughing at?

Something funny? Something funny about my family dying at war. My heritage?

JOHNJOE: Chill out, Jim.

JIM: They're laughing at me. You helped them make a fool out of me.

JOHNJOE: I didn't.

JIM: Any opportunity to take the piss out of me, mate, right?

JOHNJOE: I'm sor/

JIM: /They're jealous of me. We used to rule the world and all that's left of it is my need to apologise.

JOHNJOE: Jim no one is jealous of/

JIM: *(Towards the audience)* /Where are you from?

JOHNJOE: Jim. Stop.

JIM: No, it's important. None of them get it. They don't get it.

(Towards the audience) I mean it. Where are you from?

JIM walks towards the audience and JOHNJOE attempts to pull him back. JIM resists.

JOHNJOE: I'm serious, man, stop it.

JIM: WHERE THE FUCK ARE YOU FROM?

JOHNJOE: JIM. This isn't who you are.

JOHNJOE holds JIM's wrist. JIM hits him off.

JIM: Yes it is.

JIM: We go again.

JOHNJOE: What?

JIM: We do the scene again and do it how it's meant to be done.

JOHNJOE: How many times do you want to do this to try and make it fit?/

JIM: As many times as it takes.

This is my story. This is my identity. This is my country. Do you understand?

JOHNJOE: Yes.

JIM: Good.

(Aggressively) Lights, please.

20: YPRES AGAIN

They reset the scene—Ypres. They do it again.

JIM is angry beneath the surface. Telling JOHNJOE what to do.

JOHNJOE is reluctantly going along with the scene, clearly conflicted.

They go to the mannequins and put on their blazers/badges reinhabiting JOSEPH and EDDIE.

JOSEPH: Beautiful day.

EDDIE: Quite.

JOSEPH: It's good to see you.

EDDIE: It's good to see you too.

JOSEPH: I haven't seen you since…

EDDIE: The War.

JOSEPH: May I ask a bit of a strange question.

EDDIE: Go ahead.

JOSEPH: May I hold your hand?

JOHNJOE looks at JIM for a second. Contemplates the decision to either speak up or shrink down. The audience should be made clear of this inner turmoil.

JOSEPH: I know it's peculiar, old chap. It's just that you're the only one who really understands what we've been through. If there was a way to have this vindicated, physically that is. Even if just for a fleeting moment. I'd be ever so grateful.

Pause.

EDDIE: Anything for you, old friend.

They hold hands.

21: END OF THE PLAY

The lighting state snaps back to Realism.

JIM rips off his blazer quickly and returns it to the mannequin.

JOHNJOE slowly takes his blazer off but this time does not put it back on his mannequin and instead holds it.

JIM: Wasn't that spectacular?

JOHNJOE takes off his blazer. Is torn apart by the decision to lose part of himself for JIM.

JIM: I told you the poppy can do that, it can make Britain great.

JOHNJOE: Britain?

JIM: Because they're such a beautiful flower.

JOHNJOE: You can have it.

JIM: It's everything.

JOHNJOE: If that's what you're missing, you can have it.
But I don't think it is.

JIM: They're so beautiful.

JOHNJOE: I don't think it matters what I say now, does it?

JIM: Thank you, Johnjoe.

JOHNJOE: But I want you to know.
It hurts me.
That what you've chosen. This stubbornness. Is lonely.
I've done what you've done, before. I can't, I won't do it again.

JIM: Ready?

JOHNJOE: The people who ripped apart my country are the same ones who have told you what yours is. That it's this one thing.

JIM: Set?

JOHNJOE: And it can be this one thing if you want it to be. But it could be so much more. You could be so much more. I really thought you were so much more.

JIM: Go.

JOHNJOE: I think you ought to feel that loneliness the same way that I have done.

JIM: Aren't they beautiful?!

JOHNJOE: I'll be here when you get back.

JIM: More than beautiful.

JOHNJOE: If you make it back.

JIM: It encapsulates everything.

JOHNJOE: Open arms.

JIM: Who I am.

JOHNJOE: If you're that intent on going, go.

JIM: You get it now, right?

JOHNJOE: But please come back.

JIM: I want to be the soil.

JOHNJOE: Please don't get lost.
I can't lose you to this.

JOHNJOE exits, taking his blazer with him, and watches JIM from the crowd.

JIM finds fake poppies and plants them in dirt atop one of the boxes. JOHNJOE leaves as this starts.

JIM rubs dirt and blood into his chest to form an abstract poppy.

JIM: What do you think of that, Johnjoe?

JOHNJOE:

JIM: Isn't that beautiful imagery? I'll be the soil for a beautiful poppy.

JOHNJOE:

JIM: And they'll grow all over England. All year round.

JOHNJOE:

JIM: And we'll all celebrate them.

JOHNJOE:

JIM: Because they're so beautiful.

JOHNJOE:

JIM: Don't you think they're beautiful?

JOHNJOE:

The poppy is fully formed by JIM's rubbing of dirt and blood on his chest. It hurts.

JIM: They're so beautiful.

Lights down.

END

ALSO AVAILABLE FROM SALAMANDER STREET

All Salamander Street plays can be bought in bulk at a discount for performance or study. Contact info@salamanderstreet.com to enquire about performance licenses.

EAT THE RICH (but maybe not me mates x)
by Jade Franks
ISBN: 9781068233449

Witty, provocative and utterly current—a bold exploration of class, privilege and power from one of the UK's most exciting new playwrights.

THE OLIVE BOY
by Ollie Maddigan
ISBN: 9781068233487

Based on his real life story, Ollie Maddigan's Offie-winning solo show introduces The Olive Boy. Forced to change schools and move in with a man he barely knows, The Olive Boy is attempting to stay sane and finally get a real girlfriend.

ATHENS OF THE NORTH
by Mark Hannah
ISBN: 9781068233425

A love letter tae Edinburgh… past, present… and future.

DEAD SHEEP
by Johnathan Maitland
ISBN: 9781913630782

A comedy drama about sacked Foreign Secretary Geoffrey Howe who overcame his limitations to destroy Margaret Thatcher with one of history's great political speeches.

NOWHERE by Khalid Abdalla
ISBN: 9781068696251

Khalid Abdalla's surprising solo show about his own history and involvement in the Egyptian revolution of 2011.

www.salamanderstreet.com

www.ingramcontent.com/pod-product-compliance
Lightning Source LLC
La Vergne TN
LVHW050940080826
845145LV00004B/1336

* 9 7 8 1 0 6 6 6 2 2 9 2 4 *